'MY MOST EMBARRASSING MOMENT'

Editor
Eleanor Jacobs

Layout and Design
Lori Abramowski

Cover Design and Cartoons
Dave Carpenter

Production
**Sally Manich, Ellen Lloyd
Tom La Fleur, Henry de Fiebre**

International Standard Book Number 0-89821-073-9
Library of Congress Catalog Card Number 86-61011
© 1992, Reiman Publications, L.P.
P.O. Box 612, Milwaukee, Wisconsin 53201
All rights reserved. Printed in U.S.A.

Table of
CONTENTS

A Squirt in Time

Margie Mohr of Red Lake Falls, Minnesota has never forgotten the damper she put on a big day in her family's life:

I was in grade school when my family finally had indoor plumbing installed. How exciting, I thought, to actually have running water in the house.

Impatiently I waited for the school day to end. When it did, I literally ran home to test out our new luxury.

There in the kitchen stood our sink—complete with faucet... and even a spray hose. Trouble is, I had no idea what that hose was for. I soon found out, however—much to the plumber's surprise.

I turned on the water and pulled out the hose. Innocently I turned to the plumber and asked, "What's this?" as I pushed the button—and sprayed him right in the face!

I was so embarrassed that I ran straight to my room...and didn't come out for *hours.*

One Piece Too Few

Edna Brockett of North Haven, Connecticut thought she had a perfect solution to a pie problem—until...:

Our minister stopped by one day just before dinner time, so, of course, I invited him to eat with us. But I had one small problem—the only dessert on hand was one piece of pie!

I thought I had the solution, however. I took my husband aside, explained the situation to him and made sure he understood he was to say he didn't want dessert when I asked.

Well, the meal went just fine, and when dessert time rolled around I offered pie. But the minister said everything had tasted so good that he was full and would pass up dessert. Hearing this, my husband decided it was okay to have the only piece of pie in the house.

I served the pie to my husband—relieved that I'd avoided an embarrassing situation. But after my husband had taken only a couple bites, the minister said, "You know, that pie looks so good, I've changed my mind. I do believe I'll try a piece, too."

I could have gone right through the floor! Mightily embarrassed, I confessed the true situation—and the minister, a good sport, just rolled with laughter.

She Felt Fuelish

Helen A. Moore of Anson, Maine filled up on embarrassment on a trip to the local gas station:

I stopped at our local station to have the pickup's gas tank filled and, after signing the sales slip, went on my way. Soon I noticed something odd—everyone I passed was waving at me. "This sure is a friendly town," I thought to myself as I waved back to them all.

But when I finally parked the pickup and hopped out, I got a much bigger surprise than all those unexpected waves—hanging from my gas tank was the gas nozzle with *10 ft.* of rubber hose dragging behind. I'd just assumed that the station attendant had removed that nozzle from my truck. Wrong!

How do you explain something like that? I didn't. I was so embarrassed I parked far away from the gas station and slid down into the seat while my *husband* returned that nozzle and hose!

You 'Auto' Look First!

Darla Wheeler of Moiese, Montana tells "a good one" on her mother:

Once when Mom and Dad were in town to pick up a few things, Mom decided to have an ice cream cone. Dad waited in the car outside the drugstore while she ran in.

When Mom came back out, she climbed into the car with her cone and said, "Well, let's hit the road, honey."

But, to her surprise, a strange man answered...she was in the wrong car!

Dad had driven down the street to the hardware store, and another car the same color had pulled into his space. Mom apologized and left with a red face.

Dad thought it was really funny...but he didn't start laughing until Mom cooled off a little bit!

Can You Crash Church?

Nearly 30 years ago Mrs. William Erpelding made folks take notice at the small Iowa church she and her family attended:

It was Easter Sunday and First Communion for our older children ...a serious occasion for all of us. My husband and I had chosen seats in the back of the church, hoping our wiggly 2-year-old wouldn't bother the congregation. As it turned out, *he* was the least of our worries.

At that time our church had those old wooden theater seats that tipped up and down. In the middle of the sermon, a crash echoed through the quiet church…and suddenly I sank to the floor with my broken church seat wrapped around me!

The whole congregation quickly turned to look, and, face blazing red, I quickly moved to the adjoining seat. But no sooner had I sat down than—*crash*…down came the second seat!

By this time, my husband wasn't sure he wanted to be seen with me. He swooped up our 2-year-old and disappeared outside. I stayed behind—and prayed I wouldn't ever be unseated again!

Potent Ice Cream

On a hot summer day in Leasburg, North Carolina, Wilma Newman cranked up a batch of homemade vanilla ice cream for some guests. Her ingredients were from scratch:

The ice cream was delicious—smooth and creamy…but for some reason it seemed to taste more like caramel than vanilla.

I went to the cupboard to check on that vanilla, and I discovered that I'd added a few drops of poison ivy lotion instead of vanilla!

A quick phone call to the doctor assured everyone that they'd be all right.

"Next time, though," the doctor urged, "put the poison ivy lotion *on* you—not *in* you!"

Anyone for a Swim?

Most cooling dips are refreshing, but this Wisconsin farm woman's turned her face blazing red:

It was my birthday, and friends and family had gathered on our Wisconsin farm for a big barbecue and party. This was my special day—I had on a beautiful party dress I'd worked on for a month, and I had my hair done up in ringlets. If I do say so myself, I looked quite nice.

The party was well under way, and I felt all eyes were on me. What I *didn't* see was that my billy goat had somehow escaped

7

his pen and joined the party. I was standing by the water trough when that goat butted me from behind—right into the trough! The party really picked up then. Everyone *was* watching me—and laughing, clapping and whistling as I struggled to my feet, soaked through and through!

Puller-Pullee Predicament

Mrs. Don Bahn of Manson, Iowa found herself in the driver's seat but spinning her wheels:

I was busy in the house getting several different jobs started when I heard those dreaded words—"Honey, I need a pull!"

A wagon loaded with grain had settled overnight, and my hubby had been trying to pull it with a 4-wheel-drive pickup but was having no luck.

I donned my farmer clothes and hopped on the skid steer loader to give him that extra "umph" he needed. No good—not enough power. The pickup wheels just spun and the wagon didn't move.

The next step was to find a tractor...but the main tractor was at the other farm, and the only one available was the big tractor, equipped with duals and hooked up to a 20-ft. disk. Hubby certainly wasn't about to trust me with *that* rig, so he told me to hop in the pickup.

Now, my job has always been that of the "puller", so I panicked at the thought of being the "pullee". But, trying to be a helpful wife, I climbed into the pickup and listened carefully to his directions.

The main guide I heard was "ease it out". After a few minutes, we had our hand signals in order, and he took off slowly. I eased the clutch out—and SNAP, the chain between the tractor and the pickup *broke*.

Hubby calmly replaced the chain, and we started all over, hand signals and all. I dutifully eased it out—and SNAP, the chain broke again.

This time, hubby wasn't so calm. He welded the chain and came back to the truck, frustrated and red-faced. "Spin the wheels," he nearly screamed.

It was at this point, having worked with my husband for 20 years, that I knew now was the time to put those jobs I'd started back home out of my mind and concentrate on the task at hand.

I made a few routine checks: the truck was running, the emergency brake was off. Then I discovered the problem—my gear shift was not in the first position as it was supposed to be...it was in *reverse!*

"Heaven help me!" I thought. I quickly—and I mean *quickly*—put that truck into first gear. Needless to say, we eased right out with no trouble.

We're not the type of couple to keep things from each other, so that evening I told my husband what had caused the problem. We both had a good laugh—and he hasn't let me forget it yet!

Mirror, Mirror, on the Wall

Irene Smith of Charlotte, Michigan was shocked—and embarrassed —to discover a twin she didn't know she had:

I was attending a big convention in town, along with lots of other rural people. At a break in the program, I headed for the ladies lounge with quite a few other women.

Once inside, I was surprised at how large the room was—and it seemed awfully crowded. Looking around, I saw a lady wearing a blouse just like mine on the other side of the room. She seemed to notice me, too, and we walked toward each other.

When she was closer, I reached out my hand and said, "Your outfit is exactly like mine!"

Suddenly I realized that one whole wall in the room was a *mirror!* I was talking to my own reflection!

With that mirror, it seemed as if *everyone* was looking at me as I turned bright red...I wished the floor would open and swallow me up!

What Country's That?

Monisa Wisener of Winchester, Indiana still laughs about the day her grown son felt like hiding out behind the barn:

Our son was raised here on the farm, but his job keeps him in the city. Still he frequently brings our 2-1/2-year-old grandson out to visit and is always telling us that the little fellow is a country boy at heart, even though he lives in town.

As a special plaything for our grandson, we dug around in the attic and found the toy barn his father had played with 25 years ago. We all watched as the youngster played with the farm animals and drove the tractor around.

"See?" my son said proudly. "He's a country boy just like me!" Imagine his embarrassment when, just then, the little guy drove one of his toy cars up the ramp to the milk house window and called out, "Burger and fries, please!" He thought the barn was a fast-food restaurant!

Hanky Panky

A Saturday shopping trip turned into Sunday embarrassment for this Sweet Springs, Missouri farm wife's husband-to-be:

My then-boyfriend was along with me as I shopped. I bought a needed lingerie item and had the clerk put it in a paper sack.

While we were walking home, though, the sack tore. So my boyfriend put my purchase in his coat pocket, and we forgot all about it.

The next day was Sunday, and my boyfriend was singing in the church choir. He had a little bit of a cold and wanted to blow his nose.

He was so engrossed in keeping up with the singing that he just sorta fumbled around in his coat pocket for a handkerchief. He finally found one and was all set to blow his nose—when he realized what he was holding in his hand was that lingerie item I'd bought the night before!

He quickly stuffed it back in his pocket before anyone could notice. But did his voice fade fast!

A Drink with Bite!

Unlike most others, Arno Schellenberg of Plymouth, Wisconsin wasn't embarrassed about what came OUT of his mouth:

I like to play cards, and I used to go to the home of an elderly neighbor to play every Wednesday night.

One night when I arrived, my neighbor's wife had already gone to bed. Well, about 9:30, I got awful thirsty because I'd had salty fish for supper. So I went to the kitchen to get a drink of water. I didn't turn on the light because the one from the dining room shone partway into the kitchen.

At first I couldn't find a glass...but, finally, I saw one on top of the windowsill above the sink. I took it down and ran cold water into it. But when I put the glass up to my lips a pair of *false teeth.* fell in my mouth! I quickly put the teeth back in the glass and filled it with clean water. Believe me, I wasn't thirsty anymore!

Hole in One

Bernard Watson of Hastings, Michigan has been trying to forget his embarrassing imprisonment for over 40 years...but his wife, Iris, just won't let him:

One day my husband decided to move the family outhouse from one location to another. He hadn't counted on just how heavy and well-constructed the building was, though.

With just my help, Bernard managed to tip the privy on its side to position it on a skid. That way he could drag it to its new location then tip it upright.

Well, we had it partially tipped and braced up by a post. His next step was to gradually slide out the bottom of the post to ease the privy onto its front.

Just as he started to do this, the door of the outhouse popped open, preventing him from lowering it. He stepped up to close the door—and at that instant the post gave way and the heavy privy started coming down on him!

It would have crushed him, but thinking quickly, he jumped inside the open door as the building slammed down.

At first I didn't know if he'd made it inside or not. I ran around to the bottom end and looked up through the holes of the two-holer to see if he was okay.

"I'm fine," he reassured me. "But get me out of here!"

I couldn't see any way for me to move that heavy building and set him free all by myself. "I'm going to have to call the neighbor for help," I shouted to Bernard.

"Oh, no, you don't! No neighbor's going to come and find me in here," he shouted back. "He'd never forget it. Just figure out some other way to get me out of here!"

I walked 'round and 'round that privy, trying to think of how to get Bernard out. And all the time he grew more and more frustrated.

Finally I didn't know what else to do. So I went against his request and snuck into the house to call a neighbor, telling him to bring his tractor and loader to lift up the outhouse.

This is when Bernard's problems *really* started. At the time we had a crank phone and a party line. A neighbor lady listened in on the call, and she confused things. When I said Bernard was trapped in the outhouse, and I needed help, she concluded it was an emergency—and quickly called our other neighbors to help.

By the time our first neighbor arrived, all the others had beaten him there. They all stood, looking up the holes of the two-holer, asking Bernard if he was all right.

Bernard would liked to have killed me—or died of embarrassment—if he could have gotten out right then!

As it was, Bernard was right—the neighbors never let him forget his privy imprisonment.

Swept Away

Mrs. J.C. Wallace of Victor, Montana learned the hard way that children can do the most embarrassing things:

More than 30 years ago, when our oldest daughter was 3 years old, my husband's parents came to visit.

They brought their granddaughter a small toy broom, and she was delighted with it. She immediately began sweeping the kitchen floor, in the middle of which was a braided rug. But after she'd been sweeping for a while, she all of a sudden lifted up the edge of that rug and swept her little pile of dirt underneath!

I couldn't believe my eyes, and I didn't dare look at my in-laws! My daughter had never in her life seen me do that...but I'm sure my in-laws thought she was imitating my usual housecleaning practice!

Toast with a Twist

Unforgettable embarrassment popped from the toaster one morning at Mrs. Lawrence Bruning's breakfast table in Pemberville, Ohio:

The most embarrassing moment of my entire life happened when our good friends Ray and Marie were visiting us for the weekend.

They arrived on a Friday evening, and the next morning I fixed an informal breakfast, with the toaster sitting on one end of the table.

We'd just begun eating our breakfast of bacon, eggs and coffee and were waiting for our toast to pop up, when we smelled something funny—like burnt food or hair.

I looked under the teakettle on the stove and elsewhere, but I couldn't find what was causing the smell. Finally I stepped back to the table. Just then *the toaster pops up* with the bread...and a *mouse!*

Its fur was singed and the half-dazed critter leaped off the toaster into Marie's coffee, then staggered right through Ray's plate of bacon and eggs before falling on the floor! My husband jumped up, grabbed a heavy cap, swatted the mouse and chased it from the kitchen!

Well, I'll tell you, you never saw such turmoil! Ray slowly shoved back his chair, and said emphatically, "I'll not eat another bite!" *None* of us could.

We're still good friends, and often chuckle over this episode. I know it's an experience I'll never forget if I live to be 90!

Not as Bad as It Looked

A farm woman who's keeping her name to herself was totally innocent...and luckily her husband agreed:

One morning as my husband was leaving for the field, he reminded me that the veterinarian was going to drop by our farm to see a sick cow and that I should ask him if I could help in any way.

Some time later, the vet drove up. When I asked if I could be of assistance, he replied, "It would sure help if you would hold the cow's tail."

We walked out to the barn, but as we approached the sick cow, she decided to lie down. I stepped backward but missed the aisle and slipped in the gutter. As I did, the vet made a wild grab for me to try to break my fall.

At that very untimely moment, my husband walked into the barn! He found us there—the vet holding me around my waist with both arms! I don't know which of the three of us turned redder!

I blushingly explained what had happened, and then my husband couldn't stop laughing. He still gets a chuckle telling friends about the day he found his wife in the arms of another man!

13

Fools Rush In

Little Stinker

Betty Mack of Baudette, Minnesota left a lasting aromatic impression on her friends:

One evening as I dressed to go to some community affair in our little country hall, our dog came in from outdoors. She was positively reeking from an encounter with a skunk.

I quickly put her out of the house, but the odor seemed to linger on—in the air, I thought.

I finished getting ready, and my husband drove me to the hall and dropped me off. This was a chilly Minnesota night, and when I entered the hall, I found the other ladies grouped around the stove. I promptly joined them there.

That stove felt good after my having been out in the cold air—but as soon as its warmth got to me, it also released a certain odor I'd recently acquired...skunk!

Needless to say, I made a hasty retreat from that hall, and luckily managed to find a ride home with a friend who just happened to come along.

The next day, a friend told me, "You know, I always thought you were a little stinker—and now I'm sure of it!"

Watch Your Step!

Getting to the top is never easy, as Mrs. Carl Hubert of Hecla, South Dakota discovered to her dismay:

My husband and I had to make a trip to Fargo, North Dakota, and we decided to take my aunt along, knowing it would be a special treat for her to go to the city.

One of our stops was a large shopping mall, where we wandered from store to store. When we came to an escalator, I realized my aunt had never ridden on one.

"Would you like to ride *up* the escalator?" I asked her.

She gave me a hesitant "yes", and I explained I'd ride up first to show her how.

I stepped boldly on—only to have my foot slide off! I again put my foot on the escalator, even more firmly this time. Once again it slid off.

Perplexed, I grasped the rail firmly and tried a third time. It was then I looked up and saw a woman—riding *down* toward me. I'd been showing my aunt how to go up the down escalator!

A Not-So-Swift Kick

It's hard to say who hurt more after this Sabula, Iowa farm woman's misplaced "greeting":

I was a young girl in Iowa back in the days when most farm homes were dimly lit with kerosene lamps—or "Aladdins"—after sundown. We had a long, dark hall down the kitchen, which opened into the living room at the end. That's where family and friends gathered for fun and relaxation when the long hard day's work was over. Off the side of the hall were bedrooms.

One fall evening, I came into that lamp-lit kitchen after closing the hen house door and scooping up an armload of wood for the box and kitchen range. And as I came in, I could barely believe my eyes—there before me at the far, dark end of the hall was the fat, short silhouette of my younger brother, Art. His back was toward me, and he was bending over to remove his overshoes.

What luck! It just so happened I was "good and mad" at Art— he'd sneaked off after supper to do some sledding on the frozen pond, and I'd had to help with the supper dishes and do his chores, too. Here was my chance to get even!

I quietly slipped up behind him and delivered a kick to the seat of his upturned pants. How satisfying—but only for the briefest moment. To my horror, instead of Art's voice in response, I heard an "Ow" come groaning out in a strong, Swedish accent.

That dim figure wasn't Art at all, I suddenly realized—it was "Shorty", the neighbor's hired man, who liked to come over after work to play cards with my father!

I quickly ducked into Ma's bedroom before Shorty could turn around. But later I couldn't resist telling Pa and Ma what I had done—Shorty's broad grunt and groan just *had* to be shared!

Dad apologized for me the next time Shorty came to play cards. But to this day I turn bright red just thinking of my regrettable, unforgettable mis-step!

Western Hospitality

Mrs. Thomas Ingraham recalls when she felt small enough to crawl in the doghouse on her family's Glendive, Montana ranch:

As usual, I was preparing supper for my husband and son, but I was hurrying a bit since some insurance salesmen were coming to call that evening. Also as usual, I fixed a dish of dog food for my son's dog, so he could feed his dog when he came in from milking.

Well, I'd just finished up when I heard someone approaching the door. Thinking it was my husband and son coming in for supper, I opened the door without looking and handed the dish of dog food out.

But it turned out I'd guessed wrong—it was the insurance salesmen at the door! They'd arrived early...and I'd greeted them with *dog food!*

Luckily, they had a sense of humor and got a good laugh out of the incident.

Lights, Camera, Action

Mrs. Leona Madson of Owatonna, Minnesota recalls when she was the "star" of the small-town movie house:

The afternoon was bright and sunny as I hurried into the local theater, already late for the movie.

Without waiting for my eyes to adjust to the dark, I walked down the aisle. I could just make out the rows of seats.

I turned into one...and promptly sat down—right on a man's lap! To make matters even worse, he was one of our neighbors.

I quickly stood up and excused myself, but not before my red face had "lit up" the whole theater! Judging by the laughter, everyone enjoyed my "show"!

'Pardon Us!'

Jim Ailor of Deary, Idaho had a steer go astray back in 1916, and he hasn't forgotten the moment to this day:

I was herding some of my dad's cattle back from pasture and had to go through town. As I passed a cross street, a black steer in the herd took off the other way and headed down a side street.

I chased after him and headed him off in front of somebody's house...but the yard gate was open, and that steer ran into the yard.

The front door to the house was wide open, too, and sure enough—the steer headed right through the door and into the house!

The steer ran down the hall, through the kitchen, and out the open back door with me chasing after it on foot. I can still hear them pots and pans rattling today!

To make matters worse, as I was runnin' through the house I got a glance into one of the bedrooms...and there were a dozen people gathered around a bed, and a priest at the foot of the bed saying a prayer.

I sure didn't stop to apologize—I was way too embarrassed! But I can't help wonderin' to this day what those poor people thought when that black steer came runnin' through their house with me chasing after it!

Empty Load

Mary Ann Crowder of Appleton City, Missouri can easily laugh over this embarrassing moment. It happened to her dad, Haldor:

In our family there are just my sister and I, so we grew up as Dad's helpers. He'd trained us well, especially when it came to corn harvesttime.

Dad would run the combine, and I would usually do the hauling. And when you've hauled for 8 years like I had, you know it's best if the combine doesn't have to wait long to unload. If you're even 3 minutes late, you'd best have a pretty good excuse! Well, on this particular day, things had gone well, and I'd been keeping up okay.

Now, quite often when we're shelling corn, we shell the landlord's share first, and then shell our own. This day, when I arrived back at the field, I counted rows as I went across the end and knew the landlord's share was on the truck. So as soon as I got out of the empty truck, I hopped in the one with the landlord's corn and was on my way to town.

All this time Dad was going to the *other* end of the field with his back toward me. And I should explain that *both* our trucks are red, *both* are Fords—and they look almost exactly alike if you're not paying attention.

Anyway, I made it into town in good time, got unloaded and headed back to the field in what seemed to me to be good time. But on the way, I ran into Dad in the other truck—and he was boiling mad!

"There's a bin full of corn on the combine," he growled, trying to control his anger. "Unload it and get the combine going!"

Well, I wondered what in the world was going on...but there

18

are times you don't dare ask questions, you just do what you're told. So that's what I did.

But I guess I would have saved Dad a lot of embarrassment if I *had* said something—'cause he headed straight to the elevator to unload with an *empty* truck! He hadn't seen me drive the truck full of rent corn away and figured that's what he was taking to the elevator.

"He pulled in to that elevator, still irritated at me, mumbling about slow service in the line—and when the man doing the unloading raised the end gate, he called out loud enough for everyone to hear, "No corn in here, Haldor!"

Ever since, Dad's been known at the local elevator as the farmer who tried to unload an empty truck!

Ride 'Em, Cowgirl!

We all know ranchers have to be good riders, but this Montana ranch woman embarrassed herself proving her ability...on a "steed" of a different sort:

My husband had some fat hogs to sell and two men with a truck had come to load them. I was standing outside the pen watching the hogs being guided up the chute.

All went well until the last hog. She absolutely refused to be loaded and was giving the men a hard time. Well, I decided to help them.

This was a few years ago—though I still remember it like yesterday—and at that time women were wearing longer and fuller skirts than today. Anyway, as the hog came rushing in my direction I swished my skirt at her, thinking it would divert her course.

Instead, she ran right between my legs and before I could say "scat" I found myself astride a fat hog heading north at full tilt with me facing south!

I won't say I was as fat as the hog, but I was pretty plump then and my feet lacked reaching the ground by quite a margin. My skirt was spread over the sow's neck like a royal robe and she couldn't see a thing.

She panicked, squealing and jumping and twisting, trying to dislodge me. Failing at this, she then ran as close to the fence as possible trying to "scrape" me off, but only scratching my legs and breaking my sandal straps instead.

At this point, the men had ceased being any help at all. They were convulsed by hysterical laughter. While it made me mad, who could blame them? It's seldom that one has box seats at a once-in-a-lifetime pig and person show.

Becoming desperate as I rode another full circle around the big pen, I decided to grab her tail and pull myself off over her back. I'll never know exactly what kind of movement she made when I grabbed her tail, but the jump she made was enough to flip me over her back and onto the hard ground, with the skirt now over my head.

She then glared at me as if to say, "I've had all I can take of this kind of nonsense," and trotted right up the chute and "escaped" into the truck. One of the men did gather the strength to stagger over and lower the tailgate behind her.

Now, if you've never taken a wild ride on a hog stuck wide open in reverse, and then been left sitting in the dirt, barefoot, legs scratched, skirt torn, hair wind-blown on a quiet day, and your face red right down to the base of your neck, then you will never know how I felt picking myself up, retrieving my sandals, and somehow trying to act like a lady as I left the scene.

But I left it *permanently*. Since that day I have *never* graced nor disgraced a hog pen with my presence.

Low-Down Feeling

Knute Erickson of Stockholm, South Dakota was as ankle deep in embarrassment as his flooded basement was in water:

I realized my tractor was low on water one day as I was about to drive over to the neighbor's to help him with some fieldwork. So I stopped at the faucet beside my house, hooked up the garden hose and filled it up.

When I got back home about 4 hours later, I heard water running in the house—and found the basement 4 in. deep in water!

I figured the water line from the well to the house had sprung a leak, so I shut off the pump and the water stopped.

Thinking the break had to be close to the house, I called a plumber and a neighbor with a backhoe. They dug up part of the water line but couldn't find a leak.

To make matters worse, they accidentally cut the underground telephone wire while digging. A man from the telephone company had to come out to repair that.

While all this was going on, it dawned on me to see if I had shut off the faucet after putting water in the tractor that morning. I checked and, sure enough, it was on—I had tossed the end of the hose by the foundation of the house, and the water flowed into the basement through a window!

I finally found the nerve to tell the workers what happened. They all had a good laugh, but all I had was a wet basement, a repair bill...and a red face!

Red-Faced Rescue

Cathy Strock dashed into her most embarrassing moment—and ended up just a little rocked by it:

One morning several years ago—during lambing time—I noticed a ewe and two newborns on the outside of the field where we kept our sheep. Apparently, the ewe had gotten out during the night and had problems lambing—she was down, and the lambs hadn't had their first meal.

I have to admit I didn't know much about raising sheep, but I could tell this was trouble. How to help, though? The ewe and her lambs were quite a distance from our house, and I'd have to cross a swinging bridge to get to them.

I quickly decided to call my sister-in-law, who hurried over to sit with my small daughter. As soon as she arrived, I set off to the rescue!

Up the steps, across that bridge and through the field I went, carrying a bottle of warm milk for the little lambs. But when I reached the new "family", I found the ewe wasn't the one with a problem—I was!

No longer at a distance, I realized I had rushed to the aid of ...a big white flat rock and two small burnt stumps! Foolish does not *begin* to describe how I felt when I returned home and tried to explain why I was back so soon—with a full bottle of slightly chilled milk...and a scarlet face.

Make Room for Daddy!

Though this embarrassing moment happened some 20 years ago, there's still one red-faced farm wife out in western Iowa who regrets her little white lie:

One spring day, my husband came in from the field, ate dinner, then went to lie down and rest.

"Don't disturb me," he said, "but wake me up promptly at 1."

Our farm is on a main road, so we're constantly pestered by salesmen...and it seems they always stop between noon and 1, when they know my husband will be in.

At 12:30 or so this day, the gas man came to make a delivery, then came to the house to collect. When he asked if my husband was home, I haltingly replied, "No".

The gas man persisted, asking where my husband was. I never was very good at lying, but I told him I thought he was out in a certain field working.

All this time, our 4-year-old daughter was standing beside me, all ears to everything that was being said.

When I lied that my husband was out in the field, she looked up at me with big, innocent eyes and asked, "Well, Mommy, if Daddy's out in the field, who's that man in the bedroom?"

Her Face Flushed!

This Minnesota woman still blushes whenever she thinks of this grave mistake:

My husband and I were caretakers one year at a rural cemetery. It was way out in the country, and there were no "facilities" for visitors.

One day a minister and his little girls were visiting graves at the cemetery and approached my husband. He was a bit hard of hearing, and he was sure the minister was looking for a bathroom for his daughters.

The minister greeted my husband and said, "I suppose you have some loved ones out here, too."

Well, my husband—thinking he had asked whether the cemetery had a bathroom—immediately responded, "No, we don't...but we should!"

My face turned so red I couldn't even explain my husband's mistake. To this day I can still see the look on that minister's face!

'Show Me'

A new baby can turn a house upside down—and do the same to a new father's thinking, as this Wyoming farmer found:

Years ago my wife and I lived way out in the country. There was no hospital, but there was a country doctor, so everybody had their babies at home. That's the way our four children came into the world.

When our first baby was born, I was a very nervous new father, but everything went fine. Afterward, the doctor sat down at our kitchen table and started filling out the birth certificate, asking me a few questions as he went along.

He was almost done when he asked me, "Were your parents born in the United States?"

I was still flustered from the events of the day, and I guess I wasn't thinking real well, because I quickly replied, "No, sir—my mother was born in Missouri!"

Needless to say, that old country doctor—even though he'd seen lots of nervous first-time fathers in his time—laughed long and hard over that!

Out of the Mouths of Babes

A mom in Cambridge, Ohio has never forgotten her young daughter's innocent answer to a question posed more than 20 years ago:

A young door-to-door preacher stopped at our house to invite our family to his church. My children were small then, and all four of them came running in, curious to see who our visitor was.

Those kids sure were a sight. In addition to dirty faces from playing outside, the oldest girl had long brown braids, the second had a long, golden-blond ponytail and the youngest two, a boy and a girl, both had bright red hair.

The young preacher tousled my son's hair and laughingly asked, "Where did you *get* all that red hair?"

"I don't know," my son simply said.

But my sweet little girl piped up with "From the milkman!".

Needless to say, I was shocked—I had no idea where she'd picked up that phrase! I was so embarrassed, I couldn't even say a word.

The preacher's face was blazing crimson. All he could do was wish us a good day and leave.

Ear Flap

Jo Welch of Ferndale, Washington realized that some questions are better left unanswered...especially if you don't hear them:

My husband and two other men—our friend Dale and a fellow named Al I'd seen at church—had just finished loading a bull into the back of a stock truck. They came in for coffee, and Dale said to me, "You missed all the fun!"

Then he said something else that I didn't quite hear. I was sure he was still talking about chasing the bull, so I said, "Yeah. I've chased him around a few times."

There was a moment of silence, and then all three men started laughing. Gasping for breath, Dale explained why—he hadn't said anything about the *bull*...he'd asked me, "Do you know Al?"

Wasn't Privy

Edna Hawkins of Woodstock, Georgia didn't realize she was taking a well-worn path to her most embarrassing moment:

We once lived in a large, old house near Marietta, Georgia. Back of it were two smaller buildings—one that once had been a servant's home and the other an old outhouse.

The servant's house we used to store tools, boats, old furniture and the like. The outhouse, overgrown with vines, had been forgotten.

One day, while my husband was at work, a man showed up at our door.

"Would you consider selling that little house in the back?" he asked.

Thinking he meant the servant's house, I explained to him that we were very fond of it. "Besides," I added, "I don't think my husband could part with it—he spends most of his vacation sitting in it reading."

Well, the man gave me an astonished look, so I told him to go see my husband at the nearby lumber mill. The man went away, shaking his head.

That night, when my husband arrived home, he said, "A funny thing happened today...a man came by wanting to buy that old outhouse."

I instantly remembered exactly what I'd told that man...and couldn't help but laugh!

What's for Dinner?

An unexpected question resulted in an embarrassing answer for this Seymour, Wisconsin farm wife:

Just 8 months after I was married to my farmer, we sold our farm. It was then that we read an ad placed by a rancher in Wyoming who was looking for a hired hand. My husband thought this would be a good time to follow his dream of being a cowboy, so we wrote to the rancher.

A couple of days later, this rancher phoned while I was alone in the house. He was very pleasant, and we seemed to hit it off real well. But it was then he dropped the bombshell.

"I don't mean to pry," he said to me, "but do you have a duck in the oven?"

"Sorry," I stammered back, not sure what to make of his question, "but we're having fish tonight."

My answer resulted in roars of laughter at the other end of the phone. When we ended our conversation, I was still bewildered at the rancher's question and his response.

Eventually, my husband came in to have his dinner of fish, and I told him about this strange incident. Then my husband roared with laughter, too! I was really puzzled.

Finally, when he could catch his breath, my husband explained, "The rancher wasn't interested in what we were having for *dinner*—the phrase 'Do you have a duck in the oven?' simply means 'Are you pregnant?'"

That was years ago, and my husband still loves to tell the story. The big difference is that I'm laughing now, too!

Fast Friends!

Louise Pavlik of Chicago, Illinois had a stranger rolling in the aisle —of a supermarket:

My husband always goes with me when I go to the supermarket. He helps me by taking the grocery cart and following in back of me.

One day, while we were at the supermarket, I was reaching up to a shelf to take an item down when I said over my shoulder, "Honey, don't forget to follow me."

Quick as a wink, the reply came, "Sure will, sweetheart!"— only it wasn't my husband's voice. I turned around...and there was a strange man, grinning from ear to ear!

'Honey, What's This?'

Nora Viau of Escanaba, Michigan found herself in a sticky situation that left her red-faced:

My husband, Vern, and I were invited to a farm show with some friends who are dairy farmers.

That was fine for Vern, who was brought up on a farm and was beginning his own small beef cattle operation, but I had never set foot on a farm.

The show was very impressive, with working machinery and various demonstrations. Vern answered all my questions on everything from hog pens to milking machines. Near the last display his patience was wearing thin.

We were looking at the latest tractors, balers, barn cleaners, and "honey wagons".

"This is the biggest honey wagon I've ever seen," my friend remarked.

As I looked at the large piece of equipment in awe, I said, "You must have to have a lot of bees to fill that up!"

Needless to say, the others were convulsed with laughter. It wasn't until later that I discovered the real purpose of the "honey wagon".

That's when I decided if ever I'm found at a farm show again, my lips will be glued shut!

Old Problem

Syl Grzadzielewski of Ardock, North Dakota did some fast aging himself when an old friend stopped by for a visit:

I was coming in for dinner one night when a car followed me into the yard. A fellow with dark glasses got out, extended a hand and said, "I bet you don't remember me." As soon as he took off his glasses, though, I recognized him as Fred, an old school friend I hadn't seen in over 30 years.

The last time I'd seen Fred was when he married Alice, a pretty, dark-haired girl from our town. Shortly afterward, they had moved away.

Well, it was good to see Fred again, and we stood there talking about old times for a few minutes.

Then Fred said, "Come here, there's someone in the car I want you to meet." Sure enough as we walked to the car, I could see a lady with pure white hair.

"How nice," I said, "you've brought Alice's mother along!"

There was a deadly silence, then Fred said, "No, this IS Alice."

Right about then I wished the earth would open up and swallow me! But we went into the house and had a nice visit—though I blushed all the way through it!

Nothing Odd Here

You can always trust children to be perfectly honest...even when you wish they wouldn't. In LaPlata, Missouri Sheryl Smithson's young son set everyone straight:

My cousin and her husband were visiting us one weekend, and I asked her if they'd like to go to church with us. "My husband doesn't like to go to strange churches," she replied.

My 3-1/2-year-old son overheard this and hurried off to the kitchen where the men were finishing their coffee. The little guy went up to our guest and assured him, "Our church isn't strange—it's *Baptist!*"

Oh, Doctor!

Mrs. Kenneth Williams of Madrid, Iowa found her face flushing feverishly after a medical mix-up:

Both our family doctor and our veterinarian had their offices in a small town near us. The doctor's name was "Severson", and the vet's name was "Sievers".

I wasn't feeling well this particular day, and so I opened our phone number index to find the doctor's number. When I called, I asked the office girl if I could have an appointment as soon as possible.

She asked what my symptoms were, and I gave a long, detailed account of how I felt.

After I finished, there was a long pause, and then the receptionist asked, "Is this a joke?"

I was puzzled for a moment—then I realized I'd called the *vet's* number! I apologized and quickly hung up.

Now, whenever I don't feel well, someone's bound to tell me, "Call the vet—he makes house calls!"

Power Shortage

Peg Picke of Buskirk, New York got quite a shock when the electricity went out:

Living on an open hill, we were plagued by power outages after summer thunderstorms. On one such afternoon, two repairmen from the electric company drove into our farmyard looking for the damaged transformer.

As luck would have it, the source of the problem was on the pole *inside* our pasture fence. As I stood watching the men open the first steel gate separating them from the pole, something suddenly occurred to me and I ran from the house to warn them.

"Watch the electric fence!" I yelled as I sprinted out the front door. "There's no handle to unhook it!"

The men just looked at me in surprise and then began to laugh. It quickly dawned on me what they were laughing at—the power was already *off*, and that's why they were there in the first place!

Are You Sure?

When Edna Clow of Cherokee, Iowa was in the hospital a while back, her sister in California telephoned to cheer her up and was greeted with startling news:

My sister must have forgotten about the 2-hour time difference, and when she called I'd already been given a sedative and was fast asleep.

Apparently the nurse at the desk was new to the job because she told my sister: "I'm sorry, but Mrs. Clow has been seduced and is sleeping now!"

In the Key of 'G'

Carla Wall of Wolf Point, Montana passed along this letter-imperfect embarrassing moment:

Our church bulletin recently carried this item: The young people will be *sinning* at the Bethel Wolf Point Church tonight.

The word, of course, was supposed to be *singing*. Was our pastor's face red over that typographical error!

Dough Boys

This Effingham, Illinois farm wife's blushing blunder wasn't chicken feed:

After living in town for years, we decided to "go country"—grow our own vegetables, burn wood, raise a couple pigs and keep some chickens so we'd have fresh eggs. But, not used to the ways of the country, we were always running out of things—and that led me to my most embarrassing moment.

A few days after getting 50 baby chicks, we ran out of chick starter. Figuring I could make do until I could get to town, I rummaged through my kitchen cupboards and put together a mixture of rolled oats and flour. When I put this "treat" out for our baby chicks, they went wild with excitement, and I left them to enjoy their meal.

That evening, a friend from town stopped by, and, wanting to show off my "farming" ability, I asked her out to see our chicks. But when I looked in on them, I saw something was dreadfully wrong.

All those chicks were toppled over on their sides, chirping like mad! And for good reason—when the flour I'd given them combined with their drinking water, they'd all ended up with dough balls the size of English muffins on their feet. It took me most of the night to remove those new "snowshoes" I'd given them!

Fruit of the Vine

Mrs. Lonnie Schott's attempt at a new recipe caused her pigs to pucker...and the Perryville, Missouri woman to turn red:

When I married, I came to the farm fresh from the city. Oh, I'd visited farms for years...but I soon learned visiting a farm and living on one were as different as night and day.

However, I'd always been eager to try new recipes, and canning and preserving food was familiar territory to me. One day, while I was visiting another farm wife, she told me how easy it was for her to make homemade wine and gave me her recipe. We had lots of wild grapes that year, so I hurried home to try this new recipe.

When I was done making the wine, I had quite a mess—lots of seeds and hulls that I didn't know what to do with. Then I remembered my husband's pigs.

"They'll make quick work of this mess," I thought. So I took all the seeds and hulls outside and poured them over the fence to the pigs.

About 2 hours later, my husband came in with a worried look on his face. "You'd better call the vet," he told me. "We've got a bunch of sick hogs. They're falling all over themselves and appear to be blind."

I hurried to the phone and had just begun to dial when I remembered the little treat I'd given the hogs earlier. I told my husband what I'd done and asked if there was a chance that might have made them sick.

Lonnie just doubled up with laughter. "I don't believe it," he gasped. "You've gone and gotten those hogs *drunk!*"

Wrong Way, Lady!

A person can't take "cuts" in some lines, but DeAnn Gerber of Algona, Iowa didn't realize that until she was already red-faced:

I was "elected" to haul grain to the elevator on Monday morning when our son John gave up the job to return to school. Since I'd never done the hauling before, John was a little concerned that I wouldn't pull the two wagons behind the tractor far enough to get them on the scale the way they should be. So he gave me all the details—I thought.

On Monday, I got to the elevator, saw the building where the scales were and pulled in. I drove the tractor far enough ahead to get both wagons on the scale, waited until the weigh-man waved me on and moved right on out. Gee this isn't hard at all, I said to myself.

I looked ahead to the next building where I saw the elevator man pushing corn into the hole. I figured I'd pull in there, unload this corn and be on my way home.

So I pulled right in with my two wagons, looking back carefully to see if the first wagon was in a position to unload. Then, as my tractor came out the other end of the building, I looked ahead. There, facing me, stood a *long* line of at least 13 tractors, waiting to come into the building.

I quickly realized I had pulled into the elevator from the *wrong end!* There I was, trying to "cheat" on all my neighbors by coming into the elevator from the other side! I could have *died.*

The most embarrassing part was having to pull out in front

of all those people and go to the end of the line. They each smiled and waved at me as I drove by, my face red from ear to ear.

When I got home, I told my husband, Ron, I was *never* going back to that elevator again. He laughed and said, "Oh yes you are—here are two more loads right now. So just turn right around and go back...but watch which way the line's headed this time!"

Most of the time I love being a farm wife. But that's one time I didn't like it at all!

Meaty Mistake

Mrs. Arthur Howell of Tyrone, New York will never forget her most memorable—and embarrassing—threshing day from more than 50 years ago:

When my husband and I started farming, there were few tractors or combines, so neighbors worked together at grain-threshing time.

Back in those days, a farm wife worked hard to put on a good meal the day the threshers were at her place—preparing an inviting meal was important to her reputation. My turn finally came.

While the pies were still in the oven, I sliced the meat and put it in the warmer on the old wood stove. Then I mashed the potatoes, made the gravy and set the table.

When the men came in, everything was ready. The meal seemed to go along smoothly, and before long I was cutting the pies for dessert. I felt *very* satisfied.

Soon the men headed back out to the barn, and I started cleaning up. I was quite proud of the dinner I'd made...until I opened the warmer and spotted the meat. I'd completely forgotten to put it on the table!

At first I wanted to cry, but then I decided to take the platter out to the barn—mainly to show the men that I *did* have meat to serve!

Later I asked my husband why he hadn't said anything when I'd failed to serve any meat. He replied, "I thought maybe you'd burned the meat, and I didn't want to embarrass you in front of the neighbors."

For years afterward, one neighbor wouldn't let me forget my embarrassing moment. Each threshing day at our farm I could count on him to ask the same question..."Are you going to let us have meat today?"

The Road Not Taken

Janna Horsch of Foosland, Illinois has been married to her farmer for over 4 years...and has been driven to embarrassment more than a few times along the way. But the moment she remembers best— or worst—happened before she was married:

Being a city gal, I could hardly wait for a taste of farm life. And one Saturday afternoon I finally got my chance to help my husband-to-be combine corn.

I rode along on the combine until the field was nearly finished. Then my fiance asked me to pull the truck out to the road so he could hook onto the full wagons once he finished the field.

I was anxious to show the man I was about to marry my eagerness to be a partner, so I climbed in the truck and took off, headed for the "road".

Now a road to a city girl is a concrete ribbon, not some dirt "path" like the one that ran by the field. So I drove until I came to the blacktop, and I waited there wondering what I was supposed to do next.

It wasn't until I glanced in the rearview mirror and saw my fiance standing on top of the filled corn wagons, waving frantically, that I realized I'd made a wrong turn!

Taste's Funny

Martha Armstrong of London, Kentucky says her embarrassing moment has been a thorn in her side for 35 years:

As a new bride, I moved to my husband's family farm. I was a city girl, so everything was new to me—but I was determined to learn farming ways.

One day my mother-in-law sent me out to pick rhubarb. That sounded simple enough, and I picked and picked, ending up with what I thought was the prettiest batch of rhubarb anyone had ever seen.

I carried my prize back to the house, only to be greeted with rolls of laughter from the family instead of the enthusiastic "oh's and ah's" I'd expected.

I soon found out why—I'd picked some ingredients for a thorny pie when I mistook the *burdock* patch for rhubarb. Even after all this time, I'm still reminded of my burdock blunder!

Tooling Around

Mrs. Ted Hudson of Tiline, Kentucky mixed hens and hardware with red-faced results:

I decided one year I was going to raise chickens for the first time. My sister-in-law was kind enough to bring over two of her black and white Dominecker chickens and tell me all about them and how to care for them.

A few weeks later, she and her son brought me a whole little batch of chickens. Wanting to show my new-found knowledge, I innocently asked, "Are these *Black & Deckers* like the other two?"

My question brought loud and long laughter, and now the name "Domineckers" is "drilled" in my head.

Who's Sick?

Toni Bartolotti of Live Oak, Florida remembers vividly her first lesson in cattle conformation, even though it took place 35 years ago:

Shortly after my rancher husband and I were married, he took me to a cattle short course at a nearby college. Being a city gal—a beautician—I found it all very interesting.

After some classroom work, we went out to the barns to look at cattle and learn about conformation and markings. I pointed to the first cow I saw and said loud enough for all to hear, "Look—that cow has *bangs!*"

Of course, I had no idea *bangs* was a disease—I was talking about the *hair* kind!

Well, my husband had to explain to everyone my ignorance about animals! And, even to this day, I can't see *bangs* without remembering that incident.

Didn't Know Beans

Elaine Morrison of Seville, Ohio provided some unintentional dry humor for her husband-to-be:

It all started when I was dating my husband, Kent, who farms in partnership with his dad. One night, Kent's friend from a neighboring farm was visiting. After a while, Kent's friend said he had to get home because he had some soybeans in the dryer.

Now, I had always lived in the country, but I'd never had an experience with farming. So, thinking the beans were in a *clothes* dryer, I promptly exclaimed, "Aren't you afraid the beans will get lost in the little holes?"

Needless to say, Kent and his friend roared with laughter. When they finally told me what was so funny, I shrunk so much *I* could have fit in one of those little dryer holes!

Fit for a King

Alma Kelling of Wauwatosa, Wisconsin learned the hard way that threshing is no time to be fancy:

I was a city girl when I moved to the farm as a bride in the early '20's. And considering how "green" I was, things went smoothly—until threshing time came around. When the big steam engine and crew arrived, I knew I'd have to cook and bake for a good many men.

My mother had come out to the farm to help me, and we somehow managed to get all the cooking done. When we finally finished, I was so proud I put my big white tablecloth on the table and set it all pretty.

Just then, in walked the crew—a group of men with grease all over them and their clothes, plus all the neighboring farmers covered with fine wheat dust. They took one look at that white tablecloth and began laughing, making jokes about the fancy city girl.

Of course, it turned out they were right. After they left, I soaked and scrubbed that tablecloth—but it never was white again.

The next year, when threshing time rolled around again...I made sure to use an *oilcloth* on the table!

Brief Blusher

Clara Carter of Ordway, Colorado has learned a lot about country life since her blushing blunder caught her short:

We had only been married a short time when my husband and I moved to an old run-down farm back during the Depression.

One day we planned to butcher a hog, so my husband asked his father and mother over to help. When everything was ready,

36

my father-in-law picked up the .22 rifle, and, after checking it out, yelled, "Bring me some shorts."

I ran to the house and got a pair of my husband's shorts, although I couldn't imagine what my father-in-law wanted with them. When I came back out carrying those shorts, everyone doubled over laughing.

That's when I learned that .22-caliber rifle shells come in different sizes—short and long. My father-in-law had wanted .22 *short* shells!

To this day, the favorite saying in our family when tensions are running high is "Bring me some shorts!"

'Show Me the Way...'

Home may be where the heart is... but first you have to find it, as Betty De Boef of New Sharon, Iowa blushingly discovered:

I was a new bride who'd never paid much attention to where we were going when someone else was driving. So I didn't know all the details of finding my new home.

Shortly after we moved in, my farmer husband wanted to go to town to pick up his new tractor. We drove into town together, and he got the tractor and started driving it home, leaving me to drive the car home.

I knew the general direction home, so I took the proper highway out of town. But about 3 or 4 miles out of town, it suddenly dawned on me that I didn't know *exactly* where it was I lived!

I thought maybe I'd driven past the road I was supposed to turn off on, so, seeing a house nearby, I swung into the driveway to turn around. Two men began walking from the house to my car.

In my embarrassment, I backed out of the drive and sped away, not even bothering to give a wave. (Worse, I later found out the men were friends of my husband.)

I drove back a few miles on the highway, but then I realized I was getting too close to town. So I turned off on a side road, praying it was the right one.

Alas, the house I came to didn't look the least bit familiar— but I decided to stop and ask for directions.

When I knocked on the door, a man answered—and it suddenly occurred to me it would seem a little strange to ask where *I* lived. So instead I asked where my landlord, whose house was next door to ours, lived.

The man immediately burst out laughing and said, "I know who you are! You're Harold De Boef's wife!"

Well, I finally located my house. But even now, years later, if I ever tease someone, I'm reminded that once I couldn't even find my way home!

Stop That Bike!

Hogs, cows, horses and goats aren't the only things that can run away on a farm, as this Yamhill, Oregon farm wife discovered:

One evening, my sister and I were sitting on the porch, wondering where our husbands and children were, when our flatbed truck with the hay racks came up the drive and into the turnaround right in front of the house.

Our two husbands and kids began piling out and started unloading *five new motorcycles*—one for each child. They then eagerly called for us to come and admire their new "toys".

My sister and I made our way off the porch, around the farm pickup (the one with the steel-reinforced winch dead-center on the front) and past the hay truck to the lineup of children astride their motorbikes, radiant faces beaming from their helmet-clad heads.

By early the next morning, the bikes had been washed, waxed and buffed to a satin sheen—but with everyone else off doing chores, my sister and I were soon deserted again.

We were sitting in the dining room with our coffee, admiring the colorful display of motorcycles lined up near the pickup. I can't remember which one of us had the brilliant idea, but we suddenly decided we'd enjoy a quick ride on one of the bikes while no one else was around to laugh at us.

So out we went. We figured that if we could drive tractor, bale hay and do all those other things that farm and ranch wives find themselves doing, then slowly riding around the driveway on a little motorcycle should be a snap.

We couldn't get either of the two smallest bikes started. We tried everything, and nothing worked. What do you do then? Read the directions, of course! So, after retrieving a manual from the house, we finally got one of the larger bikes started—it was a beautiful blue one belonging to my 12-year-old son.

"I think I've got the hang of it," my sister called out as she turned her attention to one of the smaller bikes.

I sat patiently on the big blue one as it idled quietly. As sister dear continued to have problems, I turned around to offer her some "helpful" advice when—for whatever reason—the cycle I was sitting on took off out from under me!

I was shocked, of course, but I recovered and started racing after it, trying to catch up to it and stop it.

Remember my mentioning the pickup truck...the one with the winch? Well, before I could grab ahold of that runaway cycle, it hit the winch on that truck dead-center!

By this time I'd caught up with the cycle, and, not knowing what else to do, I dug in my heels and pulled the cycle back. Now, do you know anything about hand controls on a motorcycle? I didn't! When you pull back on those handlebars, you end up giving the cycle *more* power. Well, that bike ended up hitting that winch *five times*, each time curling and accordion-pleating the fender a little more, before it finally and mercifully stalled.

When that cycle came to rest—flat tire and all (all this had taken only a minute, but it seemed like *years!*)—the silence was deafening. But the stillness was quickly broken.

I heard muffled choking sounds coming from the direction of my sister. I turned—and there she stood, both hands covering her mouth, legs crossed, tears streaming down both cheeks.

"I don't think it's very funny," I said. "Just look at that cycle!"

We both slowly turned to look at the now-ruined bike—and at that exact moment, the headlight fell out of its socket and noisily bounced up and down. Well, that sent my sister off into a new spasm of laughter. But by now the immediate shock of destroying my son's new motorcycle had worn off, and all I could do was join in the laughter.

I, of course, eventually had to explain what had happened in front of the whole family—and it wasn't easy keeping a straight face with my sister again in a state of hysterical laughter.

It took my son several days to see the humor in the situation ...and although that was years ago, to this day he won't let me forget my first—and last—"ride" on a motorcycle!

Here's Mud in Your Eye!

Mrs. Gordon Haefner of Arthur, Iowa might have been red-faced after her embarrassing moment, but the door-to-door salesman wore a different hue:

I have to confess I've never cared much for door-to-door salesmen—but, honestly, I didn't do this on purpose!

To begin with, we heat our home with oil-burning space heaters, and periodically the soot needs to be cleaned out in order for them to burn right. I usually handle the job with my tank-type vacuum cleaner.

One day, one of the heaters wasn't working very well, so I shut it off. After waiting long enough for it to cool off, I sucked up the soot with my vacuum cleaner.

All of a sudden I smelled smoke—and realized it was coming from *inside* the vacuum. So I rushed outside with the machine and pried it open.

I quickly discovered there had still been a hot coal in the heater when I began cleaning it out, and it had burned a hole in the vacuum's cloth bag. Concerned that the vacuum's motor had gotten too hot and might be ruined, I attached the vacuum hose to the "blow out" end rather than the "blow in" end and cleared out the machine.

Luck was with me and everything seemed to be okay. Only the vacuum's cloth bag needed to be replaced, so I put the vacuum away in the closet.

Several days later a door-to-door vacuum cleaner salesman stopped at our house. I told him about my experience with the hot coal of a few days before and asked for a new cloth bag. But this salesman—no doubt hoping to sell me a whole new vacuum cleaner—said he was worried that the motor had been ruined.

I assured him the motor was fine, but he was persistent, so I finally brought the vacuum out of the closet to prove to him everything was okay.

Then it happened. Just as I plugged the machine in, the salesman picked up the nozzle of the hose...and WHOOSH—all of a sudden his face was coal black!

Too late I discovered I still had the hose hooked up to the "blow out" end—and apparently a wad of soot had settled in the hose and was just waiting for a chance like this to escape!

The poor salesman just stood there, holding on to the nozzle with one hand and wiping his face and hair with the other.

Fighting back the laughter, I shut the vacuum off and directed him to our bathroom. When he'd finally washed all that soot off, he went outside to his van and got me a new vacuum bag—not another word was said about the motor being ruined. And he never returned to our farm!

Been Married Long?

Mildred Nelson of Leavenworth, Washington recalls her most embarrassing moment as though it were yesterday—even though it's already seen a golden anniversary:

My husband, our four children and I attended a lovely wedding and reception for a friend's daughter. As the bride and groom danced the *Moonlight Waltz*, the scene was just beautiful.

But the romantic spell was soon broken by our young daughter. She jumped off the bench we were all sitting on, turned to her father and me and, in a voice all could hear, boomed, "Mama, Daddy...they're so pretty together—when are *you* going to get married?"

As everyone in the hall turned to look at us, I'm sure our faces shone brighter than the moon itself!

Rx for Red Face

Some pills are harder to swallow than others, this Spencer, Iowa farm wife learned long ago:

When we were first married—nearly 40 years ago—my husband and I lived in an ancient farmhouse with an old-fashioned icebox sitting on the back porch.

One day while I was in town picking up groceries, the vet had stopped by to check a cow who had just calved. He left pills for her, which my husband hurriedly set on the icebox as he dashed out to finish his field work.

As I carried my groceries in, I noticed those pills *I* didn't know were pills lying there and thought to myself, "Oh, good, Mom and Dad dropped by and left me some peppermint candy."

I popped one in my mouth—and quickly popped it back out! It tasted *awful.*

When hubby returned from the field that night, he explained through his laughter that my "peppermint candy" was intended to cure a disease I didn't have to worry about—a caked udder!

Short Circuited

Some "cattle rustlers" prompted this red-faced rhyme written by young Bruce Burch of Sheldon, Wisconsin:

During the night my mom woke up,
She heard the barking of our pup.
She looked out the window, knew it was late.
A truck was backed up to the heifer gate!
The slam of a tailgate woke my dad.
"They're taking our heifers!" Oh, he was mad!
"Turn on the yard light!" he let out a shout.
But the lights didn't work. Were they all burned out?
He slipped on his trousers as the truck pulled away.
Command number two, "Call the sheriff, okay?"
Mom found a candle, got out the phone book.
She was so nervous, she stood there and shook.
Meanwhile, my dad was in wild pursuit,
Wishing all the way he had a recruit!
The taillights were shining just faintly ahead.
A little more speed, and they'd be good as dead!
Dad was gaining as they turned to the right.
By this time, he was ready to get out and fight.
The truck slowed down, came to a stop.
My dad jumped out like he was a cop.
As he glanced at the truck, he saw on the side
"Jump River Electric"—he could have just died!
Humbly and meekly, he quietly said,
"Is the power back on...or should I go back to bed?"

(You see the Burches' electric power had gone out while they were asleep, and with no "juice" in the fence, their cattle had taken off!)

Something's Fishy

This Hamilton, Ohio wife felt like crawling away after her most embarrassing moment:

My new husband was an avid fisherman, and I spent hours at the lake watching him pull in fish after fish. I hoped to learn something, since I didn't know a thing about fishing.

One day when he was nearly out of bait, he asked me to walk to the fish house for more night crawlers for him. I was glad to oblige. I tromped halfway around the lake in sprinkling rain and mud to get there. When I arrived, I asked the salesman—who also happened to be one of my husband's good friends—for a dozen night crawlers.

"Does he want male or female?" he asked.

"Oh, he didn't say," I responded innocently. "Let me go ask."

After tramping back around the lake, I learned the joke was on *me*. My husband laughed and laughed all the way to the fish house over how I'd bought that supposed difference between worms hook, line and sinker. I was too embarrassed to face his friend again *that* day!

Lost Her Head

Claudia Quick of Pe Ell, Washington remembers her mother's hair-raising embarrassment at an auction sale:

My parents and I had been at a horse sale all day and were anxious to get home. But my father wanted to look at just one more horse, so my mother and I went with him.

As we were looking at the horse, it suddenly leaned over and grabbed my mother's wig right off her head! The horse just stood there with the wig dangling from his mouth, and my mother stood there with a nylon stocking on top of her head!

When she realized what had happened, my mother snatched the wig from the horse's mouth, shook it out, popped it back on her head—and walked away trying very hard to look calm.

A Bushel and a Peck

Francis Steiner of Grafton, Wisconsin won't soon forget his most embarrassing moment…or forgive his brother for the trick he played:

One day, my older brother and I went into the chicken house to gather eggs. I loitered a bit, and, as my brother left, he locked the chicken house door.

He refused to let me out, and I refused to stay in there. So I started to crawl backward out through the small hole the chickens used to get in and out. Halfway through, though, I got stuck!

Well, our big red rooster took one look at my bottom half sticking out of that opening and decided to attack. I was helpless as he pecked away at my backside! Finally, Mom heard my cries for help and came to my rescue.

That was bad enough. But the really embarrassing part came the following day when my brother told the story all over school. Oh, did I get kidded!

Show Him the Door

Vince Sutek of Jacksonville, Florida learned the hard way a quick exit isn't always the best:

Many years ago I was a farm products salesman, and I called on a friendly farm family.

After I'd finished my sales presentation, I packed up my case and put my hand on the doorknob to make my exit.

Well, back in those days, a visit from the salesman was a special occasion, and it was hard to get away. But I just kept holding that doorknob, bidding the family good-bye.

Finally, when I couldn't wait any longer, I said, "So long, folks"—and walked right into the *pantry* instead of the great outdoors!

When I walked back into that kitchen, my face was as red as the tomatoes on the pantry shelf.

Fixin' To Forget

Anna Marie McIlguhan of Chippewa Falls, Wisconsin blushed brightly after her husband stretched the truth:

One day when a pipe broke beneath our farm's trailer house, my husband crawled underneath the trailer to fix the pipe. After a minute he yelled for me to go to the shop and get him the "pipe stretcher".

I hurried off to the shop, where my father-in-law and uncle were working, and began hunting around for it.

After I'd searched for about 10 minutes, my uncle asked me what I was looking for. The way they laughed when I told them I needed a pipe stretcher was enough to tell me there was no such thing! Did I feel silly!

I went back to the trailer, all red in the face—to get laughed at some more by my husband!

What's That Say?

Marilyn Watkins of Socorro, New Mexico was "stuck" with an embarrassing moment a few years ago, and she hasn't forgotten it yet:

We had doctored some sick cows with antibiotics one morning, and the medicine was packaged with stickers that said "Treated Cow" to put on the sick cows as a reminder to discard their milk.

Later that day, I was standing in line at the bank with my 5-year-old son, Mark, when a kind lady came up to me and said, "Pardon me, but you have something on your skirt." Investigating, I found that Mark had "pasted" me with one of those stickers!

Mark's little face was just beaming over the success of his joke ...but mine was beet red!

Skinny Slip!

This Bellefontaine, Ohio farm woman barely blushed over her small son's innocent choice of words:

I was removing laundry from the clothesline when some cattle buyers drove in and proceeded to the feedlot behind the barn. I sent our 4-year-old son to tell them I'd be out as soon as I finished.

He dashed out and promptly announced, "Mom will be out as soon as she gets her clothes off!"

Needless to say, I've taken plenty of teasing about that!

'Rest' of the Story

As a young teacher back in 1949, Catharine Strahm of Topeka, Kansas accepted an assignment in a small, rural high school...where she chalked up her most embarrassing moment:

I was familiar only with city high schools, where the boys' and girls' gymnasiums were on the lowest level—or basement—of the building. In my innocence, I supposed that the "basement" of every school housed gyms complete with roll-in chalkboards, chalk and erasers for keeping score at sporting events.

What I *didn't* know turned my face red as my marking pencil one day during algebra class.

My students had filled the chalkboard with problems. When

it was time to erase them and work more problems, however, there was no eraser to be found.

So a helpful student volunteered to fetch an extra one.

But when I asked him where he was going to get it, so I could return it later, he blushed and insisted that it was where it wouldn't be needed. Still, I pressed him for an answer, and he finally admitted he could find one in the boys' "basement".

"You really shouldn't take it from there," I responded innocently.

"Why?" he asked.

"I'm sure they'll need it."

He looked at me quizzically, then asked, "What would they need it for?"

"Don't they keep score?" was my naive response.

The room exploded in laughter! I stood there bewildered until a sweet, young lady came to my rescue.

"Don't you know what the *basement* is?" she queried. Only then did I learn that when my students said "basement", they were referring to what could be found there in most rural schools—the student *rest rooms!*

Dry Run

Even a "smart" farm woman can end up with her foot in her mouth, as Clarice Nordmeyer of Lake Benton, Minnesota learned one hot day:

The July sun was making our sows and their families miserable. My husband sprayed them with water from the hog house, but even that did little good. So we decided to wean the little pigs and ship the sows—we couldn't afford the loss of a 400-lb. hog from heat stroke.

After much trouble, my husband and the neighboring farmer finally loaded the sows on the truck. As the men stood in the shade and mopped their brows, my husband said, "I suppose they'll dock me because these sows are still wet."

"Oh, don't worry," I said, showing what a smart farm wife I was. "Riding in a open truck, they'll be *dry* before they get to the buying station!"

I'll never forget the look on my husband's face—or the color of mine when I realized what I'd said!

One Step Too Many

This Goshen, Indiana farm writer made quite a splash—and wished she hadn't:

Being raised as a farm girl has given me a good background for my work with a farm paper in Indiana. However, now and then I get in sticky situations—but the most sticky (and embarrassing) moment of my life happened on a cold day last November.

It was a 2-hour drive to the farm of a feedlot operator where I was to do an interview for a feature story. I arrived a little early and decided to drive around the area and take scenery pictures, which the paper likes to use. Soon, I found a perfect shot: a long feed bunk, parallel to the road, where a row of multi-colored steers were lined up, contentedly chewing.

In between the road and the fence was a muddy, frozen stretch of ground, but I was wearing boots, so I walked across to get closer to my subject. That was a *bad* choice—a second later the ground disappeared from under me...and I plunged into a ditch brimming with pungent manure!

Luckily, the mire reached only to my waist, and I was able to clumsily climb out of the stinking ditch whose frozen surface had looked so innocent. Gasping, I sloshed to my truck, my numbed body beginning to shiver in the icy wind. I had a pair of summer coveralls under the seat, so I fumbled out of my dank clothes (being very grateful that nobody drove by) and slipped into the coveralls.

Back in the truck, I took stock of my situation. My first impulse was to drive home and forget my appointment, but I had a deadline and hated to have wasted a day and the long trip. Besides I had a pair of clean jeans with me and maybe my sweater and shirt, soaked only at the bottom, would rinse out. There had been a gas station several miles away...

Ten minutes later in a rest room with cold running water, paper towels and no soap, I washed myself off and crept into jeans and the wet wool sweater. My flannel-lined boots and wool socks were a complete loss, but I'd found a pair of old summer shoes under the seat of the truck.

I climbed back into the reeking cab, gathered my splattered camera and a notebook and drove to the interview. The farmer took one look at my shivering figure and suggested kindly that we had better sit in his truck during our talk rather than in the drafty barn. I gratefully agreed.

I really didn't smell *that* bad, all things considered. But then he turned on the heater. Slowly, my wet wool sweater began to steam, letting off more and more pungent whiffs until it became difficult to breathe in the cab. The farmer, clad in clean jeans and a heavy jacket, was obviously not the source of the smell.

However, I was much too embarrassed to tell him what had happened. Instead, I quickly wrapped up the interview, hopped around the barn lot in my thin shoes for some pictures, said a hasty good-bye and sped off.

To this day I wonder what that farmer thought of me—nearly barefoot, with no jacket on a day when the wind chill had dropped to 15° and smelling like the only home I'd known was a barn!

A shower has *never* felt so good as that day!

Where's the Beef?

Marie Hatcher of Nampa, Idaho substituted a red face for red meat:

I owned a little country cafe in New Mexico, and I served a lot of local ranchers. But I could never seem to please one of them, a man named R.L.

One day he came in and, in his usual gruff tone of voice, demanded, "Make me a hamburger to go—and make it snappy!"

Anxious to finally please this particular customer, I hurried back into the kitchen, flipped a patty on the grill and started putting together some special fixin's. I added chopped onion, lettuce, mustard and catsup to the bun, wrapped everything up, bagged it and sent R.L. on his way.

I let out a short sigh of relief as I saw his blue pickup pull away, then headed back into the kitchen. But did I get an unsettling shock when I did—there, still cooking on the grill, was R.L.'s hamburger patty! In my rush to please him, I'd completely forgotten to add the hamburger to the bun!

I knew he'd be back, so I sat nervously on the edge of a stool for half the day, fretting. Sure enough, R.L.'s pickup eventually reappeared, and he came lumbering through the door.

"I was hurrying to the field," he told me through a glare, "and I decided to eat on the run. I took one bite of that hamburger... then another... and then I pulled over to the side of the road to see what I was eating. That's the strangest sandwich I've ever been served!"

What could I say? The beef sure wasn't on good ol' R.L.'s sandwich *that* day!

Just Couldn't Wait

M.C. Forester of Pueblo, Colorado was caught with his two-holer down...and is still embarrassed after 40 years:

During the war I operated a planing mill, making pallets, shipping crates and boxes for the Army.

I had recently bought a small ranch and rented it to a dairy farmer. I built a small house for the family to live in, but there was no water, so they needed an outhouse.

We had lots of scrap lumber at the mill, so I decided to build a two-holer there and haul it to the ranch.

When it was ready, my son and I loaded it into the pickup. We didn't tie it down, thinking it would stay put, but I didn't consider the wind.

About halfway to the ranch, we heard a crash, and looking back, there was the two-holer in the middle of the road.

As we were checking for damage, another pickup came by and stopped, and two old-timers got out. They both had big grins, and one asked, "What's the matter, boys—couldn't wait to get it home?"

After a good laugh, they helped us get the two-holer back in the truck...and we went on with mighty red faces!

Where Are You?

Cheryl Ensor of Seattle, Washington needed a truck to cart away her load of embarrassment:

Every year, grain harvest is a real family affair at my parents' farm. So even though I live in the city now, I went home to drive the grain truck while my brother, Les, drove the combine.

We were working on an unfamiliar new piece of ground we'd recently leased. But when Les' voice came over the radio, and he said he had a full load, I started the truck and headed over the hill to pick it up.

I spotted the combine right away, pulled under the auger and waited for Les to unload his grain. But after a minute, the radio came on, and Les asked me where I was.

"Here under your auger," I told him impatiently.

"No, you're not!" he shot back.

It was only then that I looked into the cab of the combine—and saw one of our neighbors! I was in *his* field by mistake!

Stuffed Shirt

A friendly Eagle Bend, Minnesota farmer played a good—if red-faced—Samaritan:

I was driving my son's tractor one windy, fall day when I spotted the neighbor's wife standing next to a wheelbarrow full of pumpkins at the end of her driveway. The field I was working lay along a highway, and their place was right across the roadway.

I gave a friendly wave, but the wife made no response. I guessed she hadn't seen me, so on the next pass, I waved again. Still she didn't respond. I found that odd, since she was usually a very friendly lady.

On the third pass, she was still there—but to my shock I saw she'd fallen face down onto the wheelbarrow!

"Good grief!" I thought. "Something terrible has happened!"

I jumped off the tractor, crossed a soggy ditch, crawled through a barbed wire fence and ran across the highway yelling, "I'm coming! I'm coming!"

But as I neared the wheelbarrow, I got quite a surprise—up close I discovered that the "lady" was actually a straw-stuffed scarecrow, dressed in a woman's pants, jacket and scarf!

To make matters worse, as I turned to head sheepishly back, I heard the neighbor and his hired man start to laugh. They'd seen the dummy blow over, and they were on their way to fix it when they spotted me running through the ditch.

I don't know who felt more like a dummy—that scarecrow... or me!

'But, Officer, I...'

Carolyn Whoolery of Santa Rosa Beach, Florida made headlines in the local newspaper and caused a bagful of embarrassment:

My husband, Bill, and I live on a small farm in the Florida panhandle. We raise a few beef cattle, milk goats and pigs.

I had a sow ready to have little ones who decided to wander a half mile into a thick, swampy area near our land to farrow.

She finally got hungry and came home, so I shut her in the barn for a few hours and then followed her back to where she had made a bed for her nine little ones. I took along a bucket of feed and a burlap bag.

While she was eating, I picked each little pig up by the tail, so they wouldn't squeal, and dropped them in the bag. When all nine were rounded up, I took off at a run toward the barn with the sow chasing after me.

Halfway through the woods, two men shouted for me to stop and turn over the bag to them.

"Can't stop until I get to the barn!" I yelled

Well...the two men started chasing after me, too!

When we got to the barn, the two men turned out to be Sheriff's Deputies. It seems there was a marijuana field in the woods near our place, and they had been watching for "suspicious" people in the area!

Headlines the next day read DEPUTIES NAB BAG OF PIGS! and described my whole ordeal. Talk about *embarrassing!*"

'Tis Many a Slip...

Sarah Ruble of Carey, Ohio hasn't forgotten the day her whole family wanted to dive beneath the church pews:

We grew up in a strict Christian home with no alcoholic beverages. But my 4-year-old brother, Danny, sure gave a different impression of our home life one Sunday!

He was a television fan, and he'd memorized *every* commercial. Well, Sunday morning at church, we all participated in communion, and even little Danny was given a tiny cup of the especially sweet grape juice.

After draining his cup, Danny loudly smacked his lips and commented—loud enough for all to hear—"Oh, that's *good* Mogen David!"

Hang On!

Memories of driving the tractor for the first time can be sweet. But for this New Holland, Pennsylvania man the day soured quickly:

Like most farm kids, I wanted to do precisely the right thing the first time I drove the tractor. When I got to the far end of the field, I raised the 2-row corn planter on the 3-point hitch—and I don't think I'll *ever* forget what happened next!

I was still young—and short—and as I started to let the clutch out, I slid back on the tractor seat. With that, the clutch sprang out and fully engaged, and with a sudden leap forward, the tractor banged into a tree!

That set off a chain reaction—I flew forward on the seat with my foot still firmly on the clutch, driving the clutch pedal back down. That, of course, fully *dis*engaged the clutch...the tractor—and I—flew backward, releasing the clutch again and sending us right back into the tree.

After bouncing off that tree a few more times, I finally got things under control and turned the rig around.

As it turned out, the only damage was to my budding ego—especially when I discovered a neighbor had watched the whole show from across the field!

Suit or Suitor?

Lynda Elhoff of Colman, South Dakota felt like a dummy when her embarrassing moment came to life:

My mother and I had driven down to Sioux Falls to shop. We were at the big Sears store, and, while Mom was delayed, I decided to take a look at some men's suits.

I found one I kind of liked on a mannequin. I felt the material of the pants and looked at the tie. I opened up the suit jacket to check out the lining—and that's when I realized something was definitely wrong!

There were papers in the inside pocket—and I *knew* mannequins had no need for those! I looked down at the shoes...and they were moving!

I could have *died* of embarrassment. I slowly looked up into the eyes of this "mannequin"—and found it was a real live man!

I don't know who was more flustered—him or me. But I do know I set a world's record for getting out of a Sears store!

Sticky Stumble

Mrs. Jonas Shrock of Burton, Ohio took the plunge 30 years ago...and she's been embarrassed ever since:

Back when I was a young girl, I worked for a farm family, helping with the milking and housework. One year during maple syrup season, I was painting the walls and ceiling of the summer kitchen.

On the floor in the room was a large dishpan filled with maple syrup, waiting to be canned.

There I was, standing on a chair, brush in hand, when someone knocked at the door. I could see a man standing just outside.

"Hello," I said, "I'll be there in a minute!"

Hurrying, I stepped off the chair, backed up, tripped and sat—KERPLUNK—right in the dishpan of maple syrup!

"Are you hurt?" the man asked, walking in.

Learning I was not (except for my dignity), he quickly turned and started to leave.

"Wait!" I called after him. "What did you want?"

His face flushed red, and he meekly whispered his answer: "Some maple syrup!"

Honest Answer

A grandmother from Sugartown, Louisiana, who prefers not to be named, wishes her grandson had stayed quiet as a church mouse:

One Sunday the preacher at our church came to the pulpit and asked the congregation, "Do you all know what day this is?"

When someone replied, "Sunday", the preacher then asked, "Do you all know how long I've been preaching here?"

Before anyone else could reply, my 5-year-old grandson piped up, loud and clear, "Too long!"

Everyone had a good laugh. But I could have dropped through the floor!

Paint Your Wagon

Mary Scribner of Morrice, Michigan mixed up an embarrassing moment for herself:

Our grain wagons were getting rusty, so one day I decided to start painting them. After climbing in one parked on a slope, I began painting and gradually moved to the end of the wagon. All of a sudden I wasn't the only thing moving!

The wagon started rolling downhill faster and faster, and rammed right into a plowed field before it finally bumped to a stop!

After thumping all around in that wagon with a bucket of paint, I was as brilliant as a new wagon. And I don't think I've been as sticky or embarrassed since.

Hers Was a Bloomer Blooper

*This grandmother still can't decide which was redder—her face
...or her bloomers:*

I was about 17 years old when my mother was dyeing some things
bright red, and I accidentally dumped my white bloomers into the
dye.

Of course, they came out a *glowing* red—which, at that time,
was *not* a color worn by ladies of good reputation! Good clothing
wasn't thrown away, though—so I had no choice but to wear my
red bloomers.

A while later I was out picking wild asparagus with my sister
and her boyfriend. I started to crawl through a barbed wire
fence...but my bloomers got snagged on a wire!

As my sister tried and tried to get me loose without tearing
my bloomers, who should drive by on the nearby road but two of
my schoolteachers! They gasped and slowed down for a good look!

There I was, with my face as red as my red bloomers in the
bright sunlight. Those two teachers never mentioned what they'd
seen...but I still wonder what they thought!

Blushing Bride

*Jay Simons of Noxon, Montana fell head over heels the day of her
wedding...and landed in something besides love:*

A woman's wedding day is the most important of her life, when
she wants to look simply smashing, right? My day fell a little short
of that.

The morning of my big day I went out to do the farm chores
in my overalls, with my hair in rollers to save on time. After feeding
the chickens and cows, I started out the door of the barn with a
full pail of milk in my hand.

I was lost in romantic thoughts about my upcoming wedding—
and right at that moment my four pigs decided to bust out of their
pen behind me.

Those pigs squeezed en masse like toothpaste out of a tube
through the door, hitting me from behind and upending me into
a freshly shoveled pile of manure...with the milk pail landing pretty
much on my *head!*

Well, that was bad enough in itself. But when I recovered
sufficiently to remove the pail from my head, I discovered my

husband-to-be and his mother, dressed in their wedding finery, standing there watching me. They'd wanted to surprise me and arrived early...but I guess I ended up surprising them instead.

My husband's famous comment to me that morning was, "Could you do that again? I missed part of it."

A Mouse of a Different Color

Mrs. Homer Caumil of Barnard, Indiana wouldn't think of undressing in the barn for any reason...except the most embarrassing one:

One cold day my husband and I were getting pellets to feed the calves. I had just gotten mine in the bucket when I felt something crawling on my leg!

"There's a mouse in my jeans!" I yelled as I clamped a hand on him so he wouldn't crawl around anymore.

My husband grabbed the mouse with his pliers and held tight while I dropped my jeans right there in that cold barn.

When we finally removed "the mouse" from my jeans, it turned out to be a handkerchief that had gone through a hole in my pocket and "crawled" down my leg!

I'm sure our neighbors across the road wondered what I'd been yelling about, but I never did explain...I was too embarrassed!

Grand Opening

Laura Cole of Colome, South Dakota says she unintentionally broke her husband of one of his hurry-up habits:

My husband, Rich, had a habit of pulling on the first pair of jeans he could find in the morning before going outside for chores.

One day I was doing mending while he worked, and I found a pair of jeans that needed a new seat. I cut away the worn parts and laid the jeans across the bed to finish up later.

Rich came in a few minutes afterward for a quick after-chores nap. While he was asleep, his sister and a friend came by to visit.

When I called to Rich that he had company, he grabbed the first pair of jeans he could find and came strolling into the living room—minus the seat of his pants! Did he turn red when he found out!

We tried not to laugh when Rich excused himself and exited the room—backward!

Who Was That Masked Man?

Betty Hale of Pocatello, Idaho remembers vividly the daring horseback ride her father took long ago!

When I was a child we lived on a ranch in a little place called Mound Valley. We had a herd of horses then, and one night along about dawn, Dad awoke to that awful sound of stray horses moving about, right outside his bedroom window. Realizing our horses were loose, he jumped out of bed and, clad only in his long underwear, went running out the door.

Dad grabbed a rope on the porch, quickly made a halter and put it on one of the tamer horses. He jumped aboard and galloped off, thinking he'd round up our horses in a hurry.

Well, those horses had other ideas—they raced to the road and headed for town, with Dad in hot pursuit. It was a narrow road, with fences on both sides, which made it difficult for Dad to get past the horses and turn them around.

Finally, after a long run, he got the horses turned and headed back to our ranch. But by this time it was getting light, and our neighbors were out doing their morning chores. Dad realized for the first time that he was not exactly dressed for riding!

After getting the horses back on our place and corralled, Dad ran into the house, through the kitchen past my startled mother, and headed for the bedroom to get dressed.

Dad never did find out how many people saw him riding along in his underwear on that early-morning ride—but it was years before he could even talk about it to anybody!

Worth the Weight?

Ralph Borden of New Market, Iowa made a big impression in church a few years back:

About 2 years ago I was called to another state to act as pallbearer at the funeral of a very dear friend of mine. But when I started packing clothes for the trip, I discovered I'd gained several pounds since the last time I'd worn my good suit.

So I hurried to town and bought a new pair of trousers. Unfortunately, it turned out, the new pair was just a little bit loose around the waist.

Anyway, I made it to the funeral on time, and just as the services ended, we pallbearers were asked to come up to the front of the chapel and carry the casket out before the friends and relatives were excused.

Well, I guess those new trousers of mine must have been looser than I thought, because just as I took hold of the casket, my pants fell to the floor! I quickly pulled them back up—and thanked the good Lord that hardly anybody in that church knew me!

Black and White—and Red All Over

Mrs. Don Jamison of Newport, Nebraska should have looked before she read:

A violent thunderstorm early one summer evening prevented me from puttering in my garden as I usually did, so I took an early bath and put on a new sheer—and short—nylon nightie.

It was so hot and muggy that I didn't even bother to put on a robe when I sat down to read the newspaper. I knew our faithful farm dog, "Rosie", would bark should anyone happen by our remote farmstead.

While I sat reading, my husband came in and told me he was going to check the pasture to see if lightning had struck anything. As he left, I latched the screen door, since the strong wind might blow it open.

A bit later, I saw the lights of the pickup as it turned into our yard—and at the same moment read an astonishing news item in the paper about a friend of ours.

Absorbed in this story, I rushed to unlatch the door for my husband when I heard his steps on the porch. Head still buried in the paper, I called out, "Just listen to this!" and proceeded to read the lengthy article out loud.

When I came to the end of the article, there was no comment of astonishment as I'd expected. "Uh, oh," I thought. I *slowly* looked up—and there stood the man from town who does our repair work!

Well, I didn't even bother to see what he wanted. I beat a hasty retreat to our bedroom. Just as I was trying to decide whether I should remain in seclusion or dress and see what the man wanted, my husband, accompanied by our dog, drove in.

The puzzled repairman said to my husband, "Don't know what got into your missus—she stood there and read to me out of the newspaper awhile, then turned on her heels and ran!"

Fancy Grillwork

Mrs. Donald Boughner of Gaylord, Michigan couldn't cover up her embarrassing moment:

One chilly night, I decided to get ready for bed in front of our fuel-oil stove in the living room to ward off the cold.

I bent over to pull down my pants when I backed up right against that red-hot stove. Ouch! I completely branded my backside with the grillwork pattern from the front of the stove.

But that wasn't the worst of it. I was pregnant at the time, and as luck would have it, I had a doctor's appointment a few days later for a routine expectant mother checkup.

That doctor took one look at me and that grillwork "brand" and asked, "Shall we play tic-tac-toe?"

Bottoms Up

A grandmother from Ohio hasn't forgotten her up-in-the-air embarrassment, even after 40 years:

We used to play on a high embankment near our school that had large tree roots sticking out. One day I was jumping down the embankment...and my dress caught on the roots! I hung by my dress, helplessly, with all my classmates standing by.

That was embarrassing enough. But what really made my face turn red was that in those days Ma made our underwear out of cotton feed sacks. The print wasn't all washed off mine yet...and my bottoms-up message read, "Hi there, we sell Conkey's Feed!"

Clothes Call

Ruth Rhodes of Norwalk, Wisconsin was doubly embarrassed one hot day several years ago:

Besides helping with the farming, I also sold beauty products to neighboring farm women. One day I was sitting in a customer's kitchen when suddenly the woman's husband walked in...wearing only his shorts and some shave cream!

Needless to say, upon seeing me he made a hasty retreat.

He'd been in the bathroom shaving when he heard his wife talking, and thought she was talking to *him*.

Enough embarrassment for one day? Not quite!

After a few more calls that day, I decided to quit and go home because it was terribly hot. Our home was the only farm on a dead-end road...well out of the view of any neighbors. And our faithful dog always sounded an early alarm if someone was coming.

So, to cool off, I took off all my clothes except the bare essentials, grabbed a magazine and went outside to sit in the shade on the front step.

I became engrossed in a magazine article, and when I finally looked up, I was paralyzed to see a car stopping in front of our house. To make matters worse, I was all thumbs getting the doorknob to work when I tried to run into the house.

After my not so hasty retreat, I peeked out our window to see ...my Avon customer's husband, chatting with my husband!

I guess it was just one of those hot days when even the *dog* quit workin'!

We Have Company!

Believe it or not, Lewis Young of Ripley, West Virginia needed more than a towel to hide his embarrassment:

I awoke late one hot July Sunday morning to the squealing of the pigs. Their racket told me I had better go feed them before I bathed and dressed.

Draping only a bath towel around me, I walked to the barn and fed the animals. Then I returned to the house and immediately removed the towel.

But I guess I should have looked first—as soon as that towel dropped to the floor, I noticed that the young preacher and his wife had stopped by for a visit...and both were seated in the room!

All I could do was bolt from the room...and then wait 50 years to tell my story!

Coming Clean

Dora Jensen of Villard, Minnesota couldn't wash away her embarrassment when she didn't hear a knock at the door:

Before we had electricity on our farm, we had a gas motor on our washing machine. We used to move it to the middle of the kitchen on wash day.

That motor was awful noisy. It made such a racket that, one wash day, I didn't hear the Watkins man knock on the door when he came to sell his products.

I didn't answer the door, of course, but since he knew us so well, he walked right in. Meanwhile, not wanting to wash another load, I had just taken off my dress and thrown it in the washer. When I turned around, there he stood! I made a beeline for the bedroom. After a good laugh, my husband bought a bottle of vanilla and sent the poor man on his way. My face was still red the next time the Watkins man called. And you know what...his was, too!"

Hide and Seek

A friend of Mrs. Gordon Haefner of Arthur, Iowa, who'll remain unnamed, ducked a caller and was caught:

It seems Mrs. Haefner's friend was at home alone one day when she heard a car drive up to the house.

Not wanting any company that day, the lady decided on impulse to step into a closet and hide while waiting for the caller, some type of salesman, to go away. (She didn't bother to shut the closet door, though.) She stood in the closet with folded hands and head down, ignoring the ringing doorbell.

After waiting a reasonable time, she figured the caller must have left, so the lady looked up, ready to leave her hiding place. As she glanced up, however, her eyes met those of her visitor—in a mirror on the other side of the room! She hadn't realized the mirror was right in line with the front door, and she could be seen plainly.

Giving her a wink, the salesman smiled and walked back to his car!

More Country Pleasers!

A YEAR IN THE COUNTRY. Each edition in this "coffee-table book" series celebrates the unique joys of rural living through *hundreds* of large full-color photographs. Plus, there's heartwarming articles...expressive poetry...eloquent essays...and much more packed into each 100-page, hardbound volume.

Keep one nearby on a shelf or table to enjoy whenever your day-to-day pace gets a little hectic—or order several as sure-to-be-cherished gifts for anyone who lives in the country (or *longs* to)! Each book is 8-1/2" x 11".

6663   A Year in the Country IV **$14.98**
5302   A Year in the Country II..**$14.98**
6363   A Year in the Country III **$14.98**
SAVE! Two or more books (any combination)........................**$12.98 each**

WORDS TO LIVE BY is country wit and wisdom that will "recharge your batteries"...over and over again. This inspiring book is filled with sage advice and age-old family sayings—the kind that stick with you when you need a lift or a laugh. They're all shared by honest-to-goodness country folks—many of whom tell how much their "Words to Live By" have meant to them over the years! Softbound; 5-1/2" x 8-1/2".

6322   Words to Live By..**$4.98**
SAVE! Order both *A Year in the Country IV* and
         Words to Live By for just $16.96.................**save $3.00!** Order **No. 9958**

MY MOST EMBARRASSING MOMENT. Order extras of this book for family and friends—at this low price, you can share the good clean fun with lots of folks!

0368   My Most Embarrassing Moment **$4.98**

To order, please list the books you'd like (including their four-digit code numbers) on a piece of paper. Send with a check for the total ordered plus $3.25 for postage and handling to Country Store, Suite 1352, Box 612, Milwaukee WI 53201. Or—for charge orders of $15 or more —call in your order *toll-free* by dialing 1-800/558-1013 (Monday-Friday 7 a.m.-9 p.m., Saturday 8 a.m.-3:30 p.m. Central Time).